At the River

At the River

Poems of Love and Laughter with God

Always for you,
M. A. Hstgs

M. A. Hastings

Copyright © 2023 by M. A. Hastings.

Library of Congress Control Number:		2023909539
ISBN:	Hardcover	978-1-6698-7842-1
	Softcover	978-1-6698-7841-4
	eBook	978-1-6698-7840-7

All rights reserved. No part of this book may be reproduced or transmitted in any form or by any means, electronic or mechanical, including photocopying, recording, or by any information storage and retrieval system, without permission in writing from the copyright owner.

Cover painting by A. K. Feria.
Registration number: VAu 1-482-834

Print information available on the last page.

Rev. date: 07/10/2023

To order additional copies of this book, contact:
Xlibris
844-714-8691
www.Xlibris.com
Orders@Xlibris.com
852830

Contents

Dedication vii

More More! 1
All Ways in All 2
Pickleball Forever..4
Double Whammy 5
Hope Up 7
Revived! 9
Canadian Grateful 11
Just Right 13
Picture This 14
Who was…? 15
Ever Will Be of Thee…? 16
Press Pause 18
A Tale of Two Kayaks: The Prequel 19
Falling for Love! 20
In-joying Three 22
Butterflies Away! 23
Friends with Benefits 24
Open Wide 25
The Crown 27
Hot stuff 28
J. Crow and the Eagle 29
Here's the Thing 30
Decisions, Decisions! 32
Places Sacred 34
Seeing Things 35
Soul Hugs 37
Let's Do This! 38
Pi Day Punny 40
Hope's Season 41
Being Neighborly 43

A. Dawning	45
Sages of the Ages	47
Your Legacy Vote	49
Where Have All the Flowers Gone?	51
Find Them All	52
At the River	54
Love's Road	55
Flat Screen Tired	57
A Tale of Two Kayaks: The Sequel	59
Until Next Time	60
Joy's Address	62
Garden's Legacy	63
911 Remembrance	64
Hear Here!	66
Happy Through the Years	67
No Bad!	69
Go Postal!	70
The Horror Continues	71
Retiring Heart's Joy	72
Bed's Ahead	74
Black, So No!	75
Whose Memorial?	76
Facing God	78
Ancients Rule	79
Slight of Hand	80
Mountaintop Day	82
Oh, We Like Sheep!	83
Dinking Happy…	85
Life Saver	86
But Dust	88
The Three P's	89
More Valentines	90
Women's March	91
Omega Peace	92
Mincing Words	93

Dedication

Dedicated to my husband, Lance "Lencho" Hastings. For over half of my life, you've "made my heart soar like eagle…"

More More!

Longing to know
more of You
Not by sitting in a pew
listening to sermons
and a praise song or two
sensing Your spirit in
times all too few.

You modeled a life for
my neighbor and me
Not just in the talking
but Your way of walking
that even those
blind could see.

Other questions more
than answers
You most often gave
so with dropped stones of
self-righteousness
a higher road might
we pave
And ourselves from ourselves
we can hope to be saved.

April 12, 2023

All Ways in All

God is good
in times not a few
though it won't
be in the same ways
to me or to you

We may have been
wounded along
our paths way
by a father's wrath
or a mom
who wouldn't stay
making regrettable
parent holidays

But consider those Some Ones
who have been sent beside
until you were able
to hit your own stride
How were you influenced
or had made your days
by a teacher's
encouragement,
a neighbor's
kind ways?

We all are given
infinite chances
to wake
from our
pursuit of the

shiny things
trances
and more thank you's
than please's say

So thankful
is what
this poem
is today

You, my friend
to the end
are in my
grateful mix, too
For all that's passed
between
me and you

July 22, 2022

Pickleball Forever

I may be considered
less spice than sage
but now that I've reached
that of age certain
and I'm closer to
my final curtain.

In this third act,
I'm not down with
the shredding
of my meniscus
Or getting
my back
out of whack.
That is why I so love
Pickleball.

As long as I recall no ball
is worth a fall
There's lots
of fun and laughter
before that run
among
the Ever-Afters
for me and everyone, all.

October 28, 2021

Double Whammy

When I was sixteen
in a restaurant I worked
for Owner Sam who was
completely a jerk.

My dishwashing job's
only saving grace
was Myra the cook
with a gentle black face.

Just not enough purchased for all
the coffee and tea
But when clean saucers ran out,
Sam always blamed me.

Still, between Myra and I,
there was lots of laughter
Until she shared what went on
in hours after.

"Sam has sex with me 3 or 4 times a week",
was the bomb she dropped,
as my heart revved and my mind went a-pop.

"But Sam's married and has kids.
What about that?"
"He says he loves me", her voice lined-flat.

What was she trying her best to me say...
A warning to fresh flesh...
Another conquer for the day?

The next morning shift after,
Sam gave me the sack.
College-bound,
I left without looking back.

Myra, though, on both sides was trapped.
She was a woman…and she was black.

April 2, 2020

Hope Up

The most troublesome
about this COVID thing
is not that we can't
all together sing
Rather, the not being there
even when a word is not said
Whether at a dinner table
or alongside a bed
And feeling the warmth
of someone's care.

The plus,
though, is
the opportunity for us
to learn to interact
with others who had
not run in our packs.

Those folks we previously
for granted taken or ignored
Perhaps those with whom
we were
just. plain. bored.

Though we may not agree with
the Others' life circumstance
They, too
are longing to
again
sing and dance

With those whom they love
So let's choose the road
inclined towards above
It is really not that hard of a task
and will show much love
to all you pass
by
Just. wearing. a. mask.

Lavish hope with eyes brightened
by your wonderful smile
And cause hearts' feet to lighten
no matter detours or miles.

December 12, 2020

Revived!

When I fell hard for You,
I was amazed
At the joyful awakening
from my sin-filled daze.

All the plans for revenge
on my enemies
Got laid aside by
Your love for me.

Whether morning or
night or even at noon
You were at the ready
for a honeyme-You'n.

Yes, for a while it was all
sweetness and light
But the old self and the
world again started their fight.

Life's busyness as up
the ladder I strode
Caused my love times
with You to slowly erode.

With Side A's and Side B's
that developed at church
I began after You not
to hunger and thirst.

Yes, I missed You some times
but not quite enough
To invite Your return
to again fill my cup,
It's taken a pandemic
for me to see
the joy that is mine
when I choose You and me.

April 6, 2020

Canadian Grateful

Summer simmers down and light short falls,
S'more of melted mallow chocolate grahams around
bonfires, all
Pumpkin Spice in every drink but that's not nearly all
me thinks
we need be thankful for
in this season we call fall.

To our North we turn our eyes in these
October days
to ones we know as more polite, if not
more wise in ways than we
"Please" and "thank you" they still on a
consistent basis say
and added to a gentle smile may even be an "eh?".

Some "Caesar" the moment
in Churchill
where polar bears rock
as stars.
Others "Mounty" up
for Wings 'n Wobblies at
English pubs and bars.

If not savoring Poutine or
my more favored Peameal Bacon, it's
Coffee Crisps or Butter Tarts you
Tuque Donners are makin'

From Calgary Stampede to
the Crokinole game
there is no viral
to your Canadian fame.

With jest being now
laid aside
you must realize this
with the greatest of pride:
You are the best NextDoors
to our North side.

With gratitude we are full
because of your nice ways
and sincerely wish
you's and vous Eh…
Happy Thanksgiving Day!

October 10, 2022

Just Right

Oh God, how I want a world
without color vs white
Where a woman can walk
in safety
in day or at night

And children go to school
without hunger or fright.
It seems hard and heavy
when Your yoke is easy
and Your burden light.

May I, today, with all of my might
Be and do
for my neighbor
what You've taught me is right.

September 14, 2020

Picture This

Any act hindering relishing the
present you are in
should now and forever be
considered mortal sin.
Before for this first verse,
you want to take me to task,
lay aside your MobileMe phone and
of yourself just ask:

Was I freeze-framed by the wonder of a
glorious sunset
or more
focused on the plethora of pictures
I could get?

Disappointed at
return vacation views?
After having resorted
once again
to your frequent switcheroo?
Ghosting time promised as
"Just me and only you"?

A picture may value at
a thousand words,
But the snap will never capture
the rapture
before your present eyes.
It is but a shadow; the evaporated wow of
the now
never re-materialized…

July 29, 2022

Who was...?

He was part of the family
for 37 years
Having the answers
said with good cheer.

Sporting a hairy lip
as our Coca-Colas at 7:00
we sipped
Then shaved it off
as over the clues we
continued to trip.

Among the ladies
there were those disputes
about the best color
for his well-tailored suits.

But there was never a question
about this plain fact:
Alex Trebek
was a class act!

November 8, 2020

Ever Will Be of Thee...?

1+1 does equal two
Though I know I can't speak for you,
I'm weary of a zero sum game
that's been played with
only White Reds or White Blues.

We are a country of many shades
But that's not how consists
the fists
who hold in spades
the power and wealth.

We 99%-er's are left
to fend for ourselves
with the slight-of-hand
again and again
we get dealt.

For those of us who are white
it is way past the debt overdue
to demand of those with the might
to stop this arguing over
Who's
the most "Red" or best "Blue".

Standing up for what is right
and that we know as true.
Ensuring that all gets the
justice that everyone's due.

It's life or death of democracy
that now is at stake
Not some conspiracy theory
or what's been called 'The Deep State'.

Decide today to stop this divisiveness
between you, your neighbor and me
And make US again

the beautiful land
of the brave and the free
so we can
all sing in truth, equally,
"My country…'tis really for All and from Thee'…"

November 17, 2020

Press Pause

The cause for the pause
may be sundry or few
culling sleep from all dusks to
every new dew
Was it something you said
or who's been in your bed
after promises made
to whom you are wed?

Perhaps the battle is
in your head
Though not caused by you,
your Some One's still dead.
A childhood stolen with no such way to see through
to justice that is
much long overdue.

Whatever the reason
for the season you find yourself in
whether accidental, unconscious or intentional sin
Tend to your heart's garden so
bitter weed growth
does not spirit, too, win.

Be still in your pain
until silence begins
growing grace and forgiveness of self
from within
and Love's healing
insight dawns for you
once again.

October 12, 2022

A Tale of Two Kayaks: The Prequel

I am commencing to yak and yak
about my love for a Pakayak.

She is red like a ruby,
which is also her name
And though she'll not bring me
fortune or fame
there will stern to bow
be lots of pleasure
As I ply Florida springs
at this lamb's leisure.

Ruby also has a Canadian sister
Who because of COVID
this season I missed her.

Next summer, however,
we'll make like two otters
"'Tis a far far better thing I do…'"
and that's be on the water.

September 20, 2020

Falling for Love!

The Summer folds into fall
With cooler breezes
for sweaters call
Green leaves
brightening into red
Remind me of
the blood You shed.

Whether I could run
or yet just crawl
You loved me then
and time all
Not Because I've done
to my fellow
humans no wrong.

Rather
from the beginning
You penned a love song
Sung into my heart
and the souls
of the throngs.

And gone viral for
all eternity's long
So what is it now
that we are to do
To keep this subscription
on automatic renew:

Love your next-door
sheep as much
as you do you.

October 18, 2020

In-joying Three

Today marks year three
of me
as foot-loose as well as
work-free.

I love waking each day knowing
I can do all my own way
with no one to say
how long on one thing
my attention must stay.

Now, it's Pickleball three
times a week and
waters for kayaking that I seek.
If it's not
Sweetwater Branch Wetlands for hiking
I'll be headed to Hawthorne's Trail
to go biking.

Then there's the
Mexico travel
with my amazing
Mayan speaking "Lencho" who
when plans begin to unravel
helps me get back my grip as I go.

As Hubby Lance/Lencho often says
with a smirk
I just don't have the time
to go back to work.

February 1, 2022

Butterflies Away!

Butterfly, butterfly in royal wing array,
from egg to flight in just 30 days.

It takes not a sage
to know
you're being
sprayed away.

Candy for our eyes
while pollinating our food.
Becoming memories' sighs
'cause we're killing all of you.

March 12, 2021

Friends with Benefits

Oh God of all and all divine
Grateful am I that I am Yours
and You are mine!

Whether adding jewels to my crown
or committing a crime
You are there in an eye blink
whenever I call.
Not just to pick me up
after pride's fall
but to ravish me with love
for eternity's all.

I'm forgiven and cleansed; that's all I know.
In spite of the number of lines I don't tow
You paid the price for me
and so
I should to my neighbors joyfully go
And into their broken hearts soils' sow.

The seeds of grace
and love clear to eternity's end
All the while I have the privilege
of Your calling me, friend.

October 20, 2020

Open Wide

These days when it seems
not eye to eye we much see
I believe there's something
on which we all can agree
And that's on the one professional
we least like to see
With any -
if at all -
regularity.

With those twice-a-year cleanings
I always comply
But I'm not going to sit here
and to your face lie!

No, the love of the drill-
it's not a thing I can fake.
Oh, to have just brushed
and flossed more
and eaten less chocolate cake.

I lose my nerve
as down the canal the files go
Like a gondolier,
just more excruciatingly slow.

In claiming as mine
a real gold crown
I would have to rob
the biggest bank in town.

I'm bracing for the day
when Sissy's teeth
are finally straight.
And praying Junior's
can avoid
a similar fate
Otherwise, it's back
to my working
overtime late.

I'd rather not become
an indentured anything
Yet, those implants are such
a chunk of cha-ching
to get them means pawning
my very best bling!

Maybe I'll solve the problem
by making my teeth,
Oh, so white
that I mesmerize deer
as I drive home at night.

October 14, 2020

The Crown

I would venture to say
that on
judgement day
there will be some
earth-renowned in line
for a.
bejeweled crown fine.

Unless,
they've wielded their might
to promote not
what is right
But ideas other
that smother
hearts already heavied
by many a plight.

Who
sweat tear soak their beds
throughout endless nights
for the fate of their children
because
they are trans or not white.

August 19, 2022

Hot stuff

Cardigan freezing
then not
Cause
broiler hot
is what
I've got.

Used to be
this was me…
Smokin' hot

Now
I need a nap
if I stir fry in my
electric wok.

Getting old
is but
for the bold
Though
I could make
some gold
off
these high volt
watts!

February 12, 2022

J. Crow and the Eagle

Only in numbers can a crow
prove a menace to an eagle
Making a unique code of
conduct and branding it legal.

From above and behind
while an eagle's in flight
The crow is quite able to
avoid talons' might.

The crow then can proceed
to peck and peck
At the eagle's catch or
the nape of his neck.

But the eagle can choose to
higher heights soar
Until the crow falls off
and is "Nevermore".

So much better than the eagle,
we have power to seek
to dispose of that of
which injustice does reek
And restore rightful place to
the mild and meek.

September 9, 2020

Here's the Thing

Once upon a not-so-long-ago time
My views were mine
and yours were thine
And how you voted wasn't business of mine.

No news was breaking
Whether real or faking
of pent-up white anger and hate.
How did getting justice for all get less important
than the location of where any person last ate?

COVID has been a cruelly good lesson teacher
affecting all lives from bartenders to preachers.
It's been a way for all to re-evaluate
what is end game important
rather than at the start gate.

There will always be those things about some
on which our nerves get a grate
when to the next gathering they come
But it's no reason to harbor for them hate
based on which candidate voted for or against
or who it was that lost or won.

We can't (yet) safely together sing
"My country 'tis of Thee
sweet land of liberty",
but we really do need now to agree
to love on our neighbors

And again be
a well-harmonized
Purple Mountain Symphony
that causes equality for all to take wing.

Hop on the Hope of Reconciliation Train
across this land of amber grain
And make walking in
grace and in love a thing.

November 6, 2020

Decisions, Decisions!

You cheat yourself out of
too much of life
when you make living
chock full of
moral strife.

Decisions don't have
to turn into a
spiritual strain
No need to be
on your knees
about choices all,
whether buying a
car, or your 8-hour call
when you've been created
by God
with a brain.

God's caring about specifics
of what
you do to
put bread on your table
is another one
of those church-ey fables.

There is no wrong path
or work
in Creation's story
In doing the most
lowly seeming of tasks

The doer can bask
in the assurance
of God's approval in Glory.

For the question is not
the what of your do
But is it done
in the spirit
of what is good,
lovely and true

Treating all along
the way
of your day
as though they
were you…

April 25, 2023

Places Sacred

Indigenous peoples had their
being in a world of God
inhaling the wind
renewed by the rain
caressing the soil
with its first massage.
Gathering sustenance from
creations around
Sharing with others so
all would abound.

The world was their altar
not any one place
where their souls got altered
by God
face-to-face
Sometimes in fire or
the stars of night's space.

No big box GodStores
built with much ado
drawing rules up for
differences between
me and you.

Stained glass walls erected
for protection
from what is outside
The very place God created
for us to abide.

March 31, 2023

Seeing Things

Throughout every season
I've sought out a reason
for my
shut-eye
being stuck on press-pause.

Yet, to this 71st date
but for just being fate
I have not hit upon a remedy
or epiphanied on cause.

Reading a Barbara Brown Taylor book
has prompted me to take
another look
at why I don't sleep
through the night though
I've tried to do so
with all of my might,
that I may grow old
with a brain that's
still right.

Perhaps it is not meant to be
within my own power
that I solve my wakefulness
at ungodly hours.

After all, during the day
with my busy ways
I don't have the time
to write even
one rhyme.

It isn't until
I am stilled
in the night
that I am given
vision
rather than sight.

April 6, 2023

Soul Hugs

Sit with me a while...
Oh, My Precious One
Before you get to work
or go and have some fun

I love you more
than you can know
So
for your sake
a little longer
just for you
do not
yet go

Into the world with
dangers so fraught
being more defenseless
than you ought

My loving embrace
if you'll only allow
Will fill up your tank
and vanquish angst

And make joyful your heart
right now

October 22, 2019

Let's Do This!

As dew fails to still
we must decide
what we will do:

Cast aside what is known
about the fate of our home?
Fomenting hate where we roam
Manufacturing ick
making earth terminally sick?

Or give birth
to a new wave of thinking
that will stop
rivers
from burning
and islands from sinking…

Instead of throwing up our hands
about the lost future of our Grands
Why not put the stopper
On the driving-thru
for The Whoppers?

Put the throttle
on single-use
plastic bottles?

Make a trip to the store
one reason more
for hiking or
biking?

We can all do some things
Like resisting the purchase
of the next shiny new thing.

Individual actions
have proven traction
to turn big things around.
After B.C.
before
you or me,
they even turned
the world
upside down.

November 2, 2021

Pi Day Punny

Upon learning it was Pi Day today,
my husband, a former
pastry chef, popped in the kitchen to say:
"To celebrate Pi Day, out of those fresh apples,
I'll make a flaky french pastry"

Delighted, I replied:
"As long as you make it with flour
gluten-free
and you serve it at the hour
of afternoon tea...
galette it be!"

March 14, 2021

Hope's Season

In hours wee
on bent knees
I give thanks to Thee.

For that baby boy
whose wondrous birth
brought to earth
bundles of joy.

The shepherds were first
to feel the mirth
about who was birthed
in that stable low.

Wise men from afar
saw the star
And knew
they, too,
must go.

To worship the Newborn King
Who'd make death
not
a thing
And love all
right where they're at.
Giving hope to The Other
through an unwed mother
a reminder of
grace's position at bat.

Indeed, it's the reason
In this very season
To live in bountiful glee
As I love on my neighbor
as me.

December 5, 2020

Being Neighborly

If a song doesn't have your affection
no need to go long
about right or wrong.
Just tap the dial in another direction.

In spite of what may be
Big T
True
for you,
it's not the same for every lamb, ram or ewe
sitting in "your" pew.

No need to "love the sinner
but hate their sin"
or
about your own marriage
get depressed
because of how love is expressed
by those Others.
Abba us calls
to love mercy and justice
for all
as our
sisters and brothers.

It doesn't mean
with my neighbor
I will evvv-er on
all things agree.

But I need still
to love them
as Jesus would:
as though
he/she/they
were me.

October 20, 2021

A. Dawning

Dark murk grey
of yet another day
Impervious to
heart's begging to
just
go away.

Hopelessness leeches on
and stays
and stays and
stays
defying

attempts
at attention distraction
chaos that curates
soul's disarray
but no
satisfaction

Until one inexplicable
unexpected day…

A.

dawning
like a stretch of long yawning
Awakening from gloriously restful slumber
dark murk put asunder

Again curious about
living's
furious wonder.

October 27, 2022

Sages of the Ages

Some wisdom indeed comes
with just age
but without a connection to the birds and bees
rivers and streams
and waving arms of the trees
There's no guarantee
of our blossoming into a sage.

Information alone
whether gleaned from a book
or surfed from a phone
doesn't do the trick
of getting into our skulls
Which can at times
be quite thick.

Knowing what is right
doesn't wield the same might
as walking
our talking out
Silently acting
in lieu of the facting
does more for our gray cells
than all news story re-tells
no matter how loud them
we shout.

The truly wise are like children in
that they act
before they have
all of the facts
trusting the practice will

teach them
what is needed to know
for growth in stature
and wisdom as
towards old
they go.

April 2, 2023

Your Legacy Vote

Splendiferous colors
shortened days
as we seek cozy
for our weekend ways.

Spooky funs' trickiness with COVID
brought special treats as parental creativity
with safety did meet
To make from nothing
some amazing eye candy
that made the night
an experience dandy.

Now, today, is the election
with the most important selection
Of a president who is
ready, willing and able to be
A champion for the Ninety-Niners
like you and like me.

For you who believe voicing
your displeasure
with whatever
by not voting
please help me understand-

How does shirking your civic duty
help your friends' future
or that of your Grands?
Be assured that democracy and justice
for all be preserved

And not just for the One-Percenters
will they be reserved and preserved.

Those who've gone before you fought hard for
the freedoms you've got!
What do you think they'd say
about your voting not?

November 3, 2020

Where Have All the Flowers Gone?

Imagining a world without bees
should be enough
for us
to fall on our knees...

Pleading for forgiveness
for an earth that we've wrecked
by our selfish attitudes of
Oh, what the heck.

Thinking only of gain for
me, me and mine
instead of loving our neighbors
and staying aligned
with
our Creator's
amazing design.

May 3, 2021

Find Them All

Every child
meek and mild
stolen life
from the wild
To break and bend
torn from family
and little friends
until their very
breaths would end.

What now is our responsibility
as the bloodline legacy
Of those who,
in religious freedom's name,
stole the land
And
murdered God's people
who were here when they came…

How can we
as The Church
take any pride
in being Christ's
intended bride
When over the years
there's so much we've done
that has caused
a rivers of tears.

How can our souls now ever rest
knowing the church starved
to death

children
at governmental behest?

How can we not fall on our faces
instead of our knees
Asking God for forgiveness
and to please
gouge out our hearts so
hardened to stone
that we choose not to treat
Others as our very own.

To have then the Pope
come as well
and in the name of the church
try to whitewash the hell
in the same
sorry game
indigenous people
know all too well.

July 29, 2022

At the River

To the River I sometimes go
my racing heart begins to slow.

Ping-pong thoughts brake; I am calm.
The living water my soul's balm.

I go to the river but rarely stay-
so much work to be done
and games to play.

The still small voice keeps calling me
to give life in abundance,
to set me free.

A gift it is; no price of admission.
There's no back entrance;
no need for permission.

Whether I wheel in a chair or the water not see
I feel the care; the love just for me…

…At the River

October 10, 2019

Love's Road

I keep finding
myself on the road
low and winding
filled with ruts
of musts and
speed bumps of shoulds.

There are detours galore
and before I ask
where to or
what for
I veer towards
the Self-Protect off ramp.

Far away from
Mercy's Camp
on the right
at the same time I fear
the falling of night.

But as all must
and ought to
be and do
concerns
by Grace are vetted
my bed is wetted
as I realize
it's not a zero sum
face-saving game.

There is no ax to be ground
No midnight oil to burn
to earn
the Love that's free
all around
and A.mazingly
in abundance the same
for me as for you.

August 16, 2022

Flat Screen Tired

I'm tired
That I am
Emotionally exhausted
From all of the spam
That's daily served up
from
that
flat
screened tin can

Why should I settle
For grazing on fake
or
news bad
That causes
confusion
and just makes
me sad?

When there's Good News
that delivers
to my soul
only glad?

I happen to have
an iPhone 7
But this can live stream
everywhere
straight out of heaven.

No small print
baits and switches
or monthly fees.
Just have to mind
my own britches
And love
my neighbor
as me.

October 25, 2020

A Tale of Two Kayaks: The Sequel

From Gainesville, Florida
across the border with Ruby I came
to kayak with Glad Klassen of voiceover fame.

We've traversed the Black Creek,
with its tannins black;
into heaven was a peek
and for more we'll be back.

Labor Day was the Welland River,
though M.A. escaped a capsize
on that one just
by a sliver.

Due to the amazing stability of the
Pakayak she was saved
from what easily could
have been
a watery grave.

In or out of the water
Ruby is easy to handle
Other brand kayaks to a Pakayak
just can't hold a candle.

Before returning to Florida
we will ply the still waters of
Martindale Pond
of which this lamb is
by nature
especially fond.

September 12, 2021

Until Next Time

As I spend in Niagara Falls
my last days
I'm aware of how I'll
miss the Canadian ways
And I'm not just talking
about the "eh's".

Not one person seen without a mask
Or witnessed anyone being
taken to task about whether or not
they should be vaxxed.

Canadian polite wins the day over might
for collective good motivates
to do that which is right.

Here lives my BFF,
with whom I love to be.
Glad she loves me for me and
I for who's she.

Deer-in-headlights-pause at
the Waters of Thunder.
Timeless cascade of awe and wonder.

Back to Florida I now go
to my wonderful family,
dearly loved, but they know
When comes the withering
heat of another

Gainesville
summer
to Niagara Falls
M.A. is a comer.

September 15, 2021

Joy's Address

Now is a good time to mend all rifts
You may think are small
But, to your neighbor, they're drifts.
Speaking of snow,
I believe we all know
of the baby born among cattle and kith.

He lived for this and died for that:
To extend grace and forgive sins of all
right where we are at.

We believe in and celebrate
His birth in December
but let us
humbly
always remember.

His shed blood paved a straightaway
to where Hope and Joy live
If we follow His directions to all to forgive.

December 16, 2020

Garden's Legacy

I'm so grateful for the day I just had
The 8 in the car wasn't really so bad.

And now the mountains...Oh, so grand!
Your inverted version of the sea and the sand.

All around me green arms up-stretched in Your praise
Cajoling my heart to rest under their gaze.

The bald eagle, too, gives a shout
causing dusk's deer to scatter about.

May I tend this great garden You've given to me
so the Grands of my Grands will be able to see
this splendid array of Your majesty.

September 7, 2020

911 Remembrance

2 fire-filled towers collapse;
horror of which there is
0 memory lapse

1 plane had in its sights
to take more of a toll
but for the sacrificial might
of the 40 of "Let's Roll!"

415 First Responders
went to their graves
due to their brave
commitment to
other lives save

38 planes
7,000 names
with faces from
across the pond
got one memory
of which all
can be fond:
The safe harbor given
by the
3,500 livin'
in Gander, Newfoundland

An infinite number
of eyes remain wet
for the regret

of that day
Mulling in our minds
with now
20/20 sight hind
are the words then
we did or
did not say

Forever robbed of
1 more
smile-filled, "Hey!"

September 11, 2022

Hear Here!

Whether about climate change ills
or the folly in taking
too many pills
About conventional or
regenerative farms
or who has the right to be
in whose arms
The words that we use
can do good or great harm.

So let us choose
with great care
the words that we share
So as not to lose
or abuse
the spirit of love
and choose to take
the road called Above.

May we do less talking
more hearing
less fueling of fearing
And doing more cheering
of all
and walk out
Jesus's example
and call.

February 19, 2023

Happy Through the Years

T'was not just
a twist of fate
Nor was it
a moment too late
that to the earth rife
with darkness and sin
The Light of the World
beamed on in.

Love with a face
Walking grace
Inviting all
into God's embrace.

May I remember beyond
the confettied end to December
Through the resolutions broken
that love is not
a one-and-done token.

Kind words just
to loved ones spoken
But to be lived into
all the year through.

For happy-all-my-days
in all my life ways
there's the Big Ask
to love my enemies, too.

Loving my way into
2023 Year New
Hoping that you
in joy
will, too.

January 1, 2023

No Bad!

In God's economy,
there is no "bad"
Whether I am anxious
depressed, mad
or just sad.

Whatever is true,
good and lovely
if on these things I
choose to think

My mind and body
transforms in
just a blink
And I realize more
than I could ever
ask for
or even think.

October 27, 2019

Go Postal!

Amidst all the mail-in voting debate and hullabaloo
could be forgotten the ones who faithfully serve you.
Those who,
through snow and rain, put one foot in front of the other
And bring you pizza coupons, and make the Day for your Mothers.

Here are some ways to make their load a little lighter
and, if nothing else, make their day a bit brighter.
Take care of your mailbox, so often damp and dark
Making sure that critters fowl can't be tempted there to park.

Keep paths to your mailbox clear of hoses and all croquet hoops
And your mail person surely could do without day dawning
to Fido's Freshest poop.
Even if you believe Bow Wow, deep down, is really sweet
Don't take the chance of your Precious Baby nipping at said feet.

Remember the law limiting gifts to $50 from same family a year.
There's always homemade stuff of thanks and an attitude of cheer.
Thank your carrier today for all to your home he/she/they tote
Then put feet to that gratitude with an early mail-in vote.

October 18, 2020

The Horror Continues

More years, more murders,
more people tormented
as white supremacy has been
unabashedly fomented.

Here we are, with a new administration
but
in the same horrid heart place
knowing full well
This is not God's will
or grace:

To ardently seek the understanding
to conquer the vastness of space
yet refuse to love our neighbors
with a different color of face.

March 22, 2021

Retiring Heart's Joy

Wondering how I did what I do now
all the while having a "day job"
only serves to make my head throb.

So happy I'm out of that rat race
and doing things I love and more to my taste.

Yes, Pickleball and hiking
are more to my liking not to mention the
kayaking and off-the-road-biking

But what's been the best
though long over due
has been the solitary
time before morning sun
And I think I need busy-ness
or something like fun.

I'm ravished by grace
bathed in tears sometimes, too
whispered direct to my ticker
are the words "I love you just
for you"

Not for my job
Not for that lob
no matter how
it was amazing

Not for greener pastures in which
I think I could or should
be grazing

But just as I am and
was created to be
uniquely qualified
for the title of Me.

March 31, 2022

Bed's Ahead

Who cannot be but sour
on this springing ahead
when we all could be
for another hour
in our nice and cozy beds
Doing whatever it is we choose
instead of a wholesale lose
of our snooze?

We are already
deprived of sleep
Due to the long hours
on our self-ish phones
we keep
and February failed to
cough up the 29th
over which to leap.

Oh, what am I to do
with all of this dismay
But to take a longer nap
than usual today!

March 12, 2023

Black, So No!

I can't help him because he is black…
He could be shot in his front or his back
I could have helped had he been white
Not my first thought when I saw him that night.

He was lying face up closed eyes in his car
Between the door and a woman a bridge too far
Around and out from the dark lot I went
to my supervisor a voicemail quickly I sent.

At home and out of the clutches of fright
I was able to consider the man in the night.
Was he sleeping…from a long day tired?
Was he sick…? Perhaps in substances mired?

As I unpacked the thought came to me
to call the police to just check and see
As I picked up my cell it dawned on me
Even sleeping while black could become R.I.P.

Three years and every news cycle I get madder and sadder
They're not "domestic terrorists"; they are people who matter.
God, Bless America! We surely do need it.
Your command was: "Love one another"
Please help us to heed it.

November 18, 2019

Whose Memorial?

I no longer believe
"My country, 'Tis of Thee"
Because too many of its people
are yet far from truly free.

As a white child,
I'd not have guessed
our constitution's writing,
some of which contains
ideology at its best
was never by
white men intended
for all who here came
to be
equally befriended.

In fact, this land we stole from native peoples
whose cultures and lives we made certain we ended.

Yes, I say "we", now, as an accusation.
Because, though we were not responsible for past tyranny's causation
It is incumbent upon us to ensure
its immediate cessation,
and guarantee that all are freed
and get overdue compensation.

If you say, "How dare you
write these thoughts on the day
of honoring our war dead!"
Remember those without flags
Long forgotten
under the ground on which you tread.

Memorial Day
May 29, 2023

Facing God

Against your neighbor
with this or that axe to grind
to God's image
you are blind.

Looming larger every day
fear puts us all in harms way.
For if we live our lives in fear
it will always be most near.

When fear-mongering makes
less of those God made as
our sisters and brothers
Casting them as dangerous,
treating them as
unknowable Others
It is the very breath of God
we smother.

A face-to-face encounter
with our Creator
we will never see
Unless we look with love
upon the Stranger
'cause that's where God be.

April 24, 2023

Ancients Rule

We have not shores hemmed by sand
Yet giant sunbathers crowd this land.

Ancient tales their flesh tells
of lesser creatures dragged to their hell.

Statues still

Comatose sleeping
Silent death knell
of lightning creeping.

Infinitely stoking our fascination
As we trespass on
the gators' nation.

February 27, 2021

Slight of Hand

Albeit appears from
the same deck
a different hand of cards
each do we get.

Some flush with aces
standard gold
with them
anyone
can go bold.

Others get
mismatched
low suits
on
a rickety table
to boot.

What is in another's hand
you just do not know
So you can not say
in observing their play
What a ridiculously stupid
or wrong way to go.

Or blurt a self-righteous
"I would never have done that!"
It's impossible to know
how you would act
when your hand doesn't hold
the exact card-of-facts.

So before you say
about another's play
of their days
What the heck!
Ponder how against them
may be
stacked the deck.

March 5, 2023

Mountaintop Day

Have you been to the mountaintop?
Or stuck in Trepidation Valley, where fear stops not
and hand-wringing and worry is all that you've got?

Well, here's the celebratory thing
on this birthday of Dr. Martin Luther King:
Just like us, he was a flawed
human being
But he moved the mountains from which he could see
the land promised to
him, you and me
By standing up for justice
while on bended knees.

Dr. King knew that only in nights dark
can you the stars see
So he acted against The Oppressor's
stark reality
to make his people as free
as they were created to be.

February 16, 2023

Oh, We Like Sheep!

In every life seasons
there are good reasons
for the way in which
Creation was done
Lambs led to still waters
in Psalms 23
is
among the many
one

You and me
are likened to lambs
because we can be
just like sheep
pretty dumb

Sheep's wool can absorb 60%
of its weight in water
before it will ever feel wet
That's why in winter endeavors
in lands Hinter
cold and wet
to keep warm
wearing wool is
the bold's
best bet

But a lamb drinking
in rough waters
would absorb so
much H^2O

without ever blinking
or even thinking
she would be sinking
and her Maker would soon
back her get!

July 30, 2022

Dinking Happy...

(Sing to the tune of the camp song *BINGO*.)

If you're happy and you know it, overthink.
If you're happy and you know it, overthink.
If you're happy and you know it,
give your brain a chance to blow it
If you're happy and you know it, overthink.

If you're happy and you know it, overthink.
Happy life will be wrecked in just a blink
You not only will regret it
You'll have you to take the credit
if you stall your happy life in overthink.

If you play Pickleball, don't overthink.
If you play Pickleball, don't overthink.
Forget the power moves
And stay in Pickle-groove
Lay aside
that Alpha pride
and do the Dink!

December 30, 2020

Life Saver

What is saving your life right now?
Being led to still waters
Lying down in green pastures
Contemplating the if or what
of the ever-after?

How about the heaven
that's in your here?
That looks quite different from
The Text Yesteryear
which dissed or
dismissed
most of humans' race
due to their gender or
color of face.

Is contentment and joy an unattainable thing
Reserved for those with cachet
or the most bling?
Or can your life be saved
by relishing what
each day to you brings?

The More which
we seek requires no
getting of a grip
Or ways of being Other from
which we must strip
The Creator said we already have
all our happiness needs
All we lack is our willingness
to embrace that Truth in deed.

Our longing for
A. Something More
is not due to our pining for
our tribe's tent beyond the stars
What is missing is our consent
to be where we are.

March 22, 2023

But Dust

Ash Wednesday is
the beginning of Lent
designated in Christendom
as a time to repent
of those thoughts and deeds
that were not heaven sent.

It's mirror time for me and
my selfish bent.
To reflect on the pain caused
by my divisive actions
My Tribe against all Other
Blue or Red factions

For defaulting my thoughts
to misguided
shoulds and oughts
including who deserves
to love and to be loved
and who does not.

I have now forty days
to reflect on these ways
To atone for my sin's pain
knowing a repentant heart
can be cleansed
once again.

February 22, 2023

The Three P's

The fasting in Lent is not
the temptation
But instead it is for
our preparation
to see clearly our
sins in all their machinations.

The doubts about
provision, protection and power
most frequently hold sway
or in our hearts tower.
We succumb to old ways
and wander in our sameness
for years and not days.

What is your something
to turn dark into light?
Giving you options or at
least some more might?
Rescuing from all
of poverty's plight?

Today is the first Sunday
in this 40 days of wandering.
What forms of provision,
protection and power
loom large
in your ponderings?

February 26, 2023

More Valentines

May we decide today
on love holding sway
not just on this day
of Love-Say…

For we will always
be taking the road
that's above
not when we
say what we
should say

But when we do
what is due
in grace-filled love
towards whomever's
the You.

February 14, 2022

Women's March

Wellspring of life
for all civilizations.
Consciences and touchstones
of every great nation

Though essence warrants more
than a month's contemplation
a beginning is
Her-story's celebration.

Women's History Month
March 1, 2021

Omega Peace

The Alpha and Omega,
One of three
who was and is and
will always be.

Took on the form of a baby wee
born to an underaged mother.
Fostering peace between you and me
and those all-too-well-known
as The Other.

In the beginning, lasting
to the end.
Not only our God,
but steadfastly
best friend.

December 11, 2020

Mincing Words

To writers and poets
who do
not their gift
know it:

May your words be sublime
whether or not rhyme
but weathering time

Helping souls climb
from lives
not-so-fine
edifying the mind
as rest it finds
from daily grind
in every line

July 19, 2022

Printed in the USA
CPSIA information can be obtained
at www.ICGtesting.com
JSHW021533130823
46467JS00002B/73